CPSIA information can be obtained
at www.ICGtesting.com
Printed in the USA
LVHW052325081019
633649LV00009B/359/P

9 780464 055143